KID CAN

written by Emmie R Werner

art by Jack Foster

Halo
PUBLISHING
INTERNATIONAL

ISBN: 978-1-63765-046-2
LCCN: 2021910778

Halo Publishing International, LLC
www. halopublishing.com

Printed and bound in the United States of America

To my wonderful family, especially Bill, my biggest
cheerleaders who have encouraged and walked
with me in my writing journey. Proof that
I/we CAN do all things with Jesus!

Dear Parent/Guardian,

Welcome to KID CAN, a 21 day devotional for young children. It is my hope and prayer as your child journeys through these days they will discover that God is always with them - THEY CAN DO ALL THINGS. It is their journal to draw, color, write, or doodle. What is in their journal is between God and them. This devotional can be used in a church/school setting or daily at home. Thank you for journeying with your child through these 21 days.

"I can do everything through Christ who gives me strength." Philippians 4:13 NLT

I CAN DO THIS

These are just a few "CAN" activities for you and your child.
These are only suggestions to get them started:

- Using an empty can, make a telephone, pencil holder, flower pot, or wind chimes.

- Take the scripture for each day, write one word on a flashcard, mix them up, and put them in order.

- Count the cans in your pantry.

- Find the heaviest can, the lightest can, the tallest can, the shortest can.

- Read THE LITTLE ENGINE THAT COULD by Watty Piper.

Look at all the things you can do with Jesus!!
What else CAN you do?

Day 1	Day 2	Day 3	Day 4	Day 5	Day 6	Day 7
Day 8	Day 9	Day 10	Day 11	Day 12	Day 13	Day 14
Day 15	Day 16	Day 17	Day 18	Day 19	Day 20	Day 21

DAY 1

For I CAN do everything through Christ who gives me strength. Philippians 4:13 NLT

Think about the things you CAN do. Run. Jump. Build. Help your parents. Who do you think gives you the strength to do those things? _____

Draw a picture of something you can do.

REMEMBER:

I _____ do everything through _____ who
   can   Christ

gives _____ strength. Philippians 4:13
         write your name

DAY 2

...I CAN be sure God will take care of everything I need. Philippians 4:19 MSG

What do we need to breathe? _____

What do we need to see? _____

What do we need to run? _____

Who gives us what we need? _____

Write two things you need. _____

and _____

Draw a picture using what God has given you.

REMEMBER:

_____ CAN be sure _____ will take
write your name   God

care of everything _____ needs. Philippians 4:19
                                   write your name

DAY 3

The Spirit God gave us does not make us afraid. 2 Timothy 1:7 ERV

There was a storm. Jesus' friends were in a boat. They were afraid. Jesus said, "BE STILL."

Think of a time when you were scared.

Draw a picture of how believing in
Jesus helped you to not be scared.

REMEMBER:

The Spirit _____ gave us does _____
               God   not

make _____ afraid. 2 Timothy 1:7
      write your name

DAY 4

God has given me a special gift. Romans 12:3 ERV

God gives everyone special things we can do really well. What ability has God given you?

_____

Draw a picture of your special ability from God.

REMEMBER:

_____ has given _____ a special gift. Romans 12:3
   God   write your name

DAY 5

Light! Space! Zest! That's God! With Him on my side I'm fearless, afraid of no one and nothing. Psalm 27:1 MSG

God made the world.
God made light.
God made you!
With God on your side, you don't have to be afraid of anything.

Draw a picture of God with you when you might be afraid.

REMEMBER:

Light! Space! Zest! That's _____. Psalm 27:1

God

DAY 6

...but those who know God and obey
Him will be strong. Daniel 11:32 ERV

Hello God,
This is _____

write your name

What do you want me to do today?
OK! Love, _____

write your name

This is what God wants us to do. Talk to
Him, listen to Him, and do what He says.

Draw a picture of what God wants you to do today.

REMEMBER:

...but those who know _____ and obey Him will be _____ . Daniel 11:32

　　　　　　　　　　　God　　　　　　　　　　　　　　　　　strong

DAY 7

...GOD leads us from place to place in a victory parade... 2 Corinthians 2:14 MSG

Have you ever been to a parade? _____

What did you see?_____

What did you like the best?_____

God wants us to tell everyone about Him.

Draw a picture of you in a parade with Jesus.

REMEMBER:

_____ leads us from place to place in a victory _____. 2 Corinthians 2:14

God   parade

DAY 8

...pray to the Father, He loves to help... James 1:5 MSG

What do you do to help at home? _____

What do you help with at church? _____

God wants to help you wherever you are.

Draw a picture of you helping someone.

REMEMBER:

_____ to the Father, He loves to help _____. James 1:5
Pray   write your name

DAY 9

It's a good thing to quietly hope, quietly hope
for help from God... Lamentations 3:26-27 MSG

Do you ever hope for a new toy? _____
A special treat? _____
What are you hoping for today? _____

Draw a picture of what you are hoping for from God.

REMEMBER:

It's a _____ thing to quietly hope, quietly _____
    good   hope

for help from _____. Lamentations 3:26-27
              God

DAY 10

Give all your worries to Him, because
He cares for you. I Peter 5:7 ERV

Who cares for you? _____

Do you think God cares for you? _____

Are you worried about something? _____

The Bible tells us not to worry about
anything because God is taking care of us.

Draw a picture of someone who cares for you.

REMEMBER:

Give all your worries to _____. _____
                                  God   God

will take care of _____. 1 Peter 5:7
                          write your name

DAY 11

So Christ (God) has set us free... Galatians 5:1 NLT

Think about swinging as high as you can!
Running as fast as you can! Jumping as
high as you can!

Who lets you be free to do those things? _____

God

Draw a picture of you feeling free.

REMEMBER:

So _____ has set _____ free. Galatians 5:1
    Christ (God)   write your name

DAY 12

Now we know this: God has forgiven those people who are united with Christ Jesus. Romans 8:1 Easy English Bible 2018

Did you ever do something wrong? _____

Did you have to say I'm sorry? _____

And the person said to you, "I forgive you."

Just like Jesus – He forgives us when we tell Him we are sorry.

Draw a picture of what it looks
like when someone forgives you.

REMEMBER:

Now we know this: _____ has forgiven those
                        God

people who are united with _____. Romans 8:1
                              Jesus

DAY 13

You can be sure that Jesus will be
with you always. Matthew 28:20 ERV

Who is always with you? _____
Does that mean when you are playing? _____
Eating? _____ Sleeping? _____
Tell Jesus thank you for being with you today.

Draw a picture of you and Jesus.

REMEMBER:

You can be sure _____ will always be with _____ . Matthew 28:20

Jesus   write your name

DAY 14

Be happy with the things you have.
Hebrews 13:5-6 Easy To Read 2018

Do you get presents for your birthday? _____
What do you want for your birthday? _____
Does God give us a gift? _____
The best gift we can ever get from anyone is JESUS!

Draw a picture of your favorite present.

REMEMBER:

Be _____ with the things you have. Hebrews 13:5-6

happy

DAY 15

We are all able to receive God's life,
His Spirit, in and with us by believing.
Galatians 3:14 MSG

We believe our moms and dads are going to take
care of us. We believe the sun will come up.
We believe we will have fun at the park.
God is telling us He is with us always if we believe.

YES LORD, I BELIEVE IN YOU.

Draw a picture of someone you
know who also believes in Jesus.

REMEMBER:

We are all able to receive _____ life, His Spirit,
                          God's

in and with _____ by believing. Galatians 3:14
            write your name

DAY 16

...I have learned to be happy, whatever things may be happening to me. Philippians 4:11 Easy

What makes you happy?

_____

What do you think makes your
mom and dad happy?

_____

What do you think makes God happy?

_____

Draw a picture of something that makes you happy.

REMEMBER:

_____ has learned to be _____ , whatever things
   write your name   happy

may be happening to _____ . Philippians 4:11
                             write your name

DAY 17

God did this for us so that in Christ we could become right with God. 2 Corinthians 5:21 ICB

Our moms and dads do things for us every day.
What does your mom do for you? _____
What does your dad do for you? _____

God, our Father in Heaven did something for us,
He sent His Son Jesus so we could go to Heaven.

Draw a picture of you doing something FOR someone.

REMEMBER:

_____ did this for _____ so that in Christ
God   write your name

_____ could become right with _____ . 2 Corinthians 5:21
write your name   God

DAY 18

So what do you think? With God on our side like this how can we lose? Romans 8:31 MSG

Have you ever lost a toy? _____

Have you ever lost a game? _____

How did you feel?

When we ask Jesus (God) into our hearts, He will always be with us to help us – when we ask.

Draw a picture of how you feel
when you find something you lost.

REMEMBER:

So, what do you think? With _____ on _____

                                God   write your name

side like this, how can we lose? Romans 8:31

DAY 19

God is not a God of confusion but a
God of peace. 1 Corinthians 14:33 ERV

Name two friends.

_____

_____

Did you ever have to tell your friend you
were sorry about something? _____
How does God want you to treat
your friend? _____

Draw a picture of you and your friend.

REMEMBER:

_____ is not a God of confusion but a God

God

of _____. 1 Corinthians 14:33

Peace

DAY 20

Because God loves us, none of these troubles can ever beat us. He makes us win against them.
Romans 8:37 Easy

Did you ever feel like you couldn't do something and everyone else could? _____

What does Jesus say you can do? _____

Who helps you all the time? _____

Draw a picture doing something that was hard for you when you first tried to do it.

REMEMBER:

Because _____ loves us, none of these troubles
      God

can ever beat _____ . _____ made
          write your name   God

us _____ against them. Romans 8:37
   win

DAY 21

Jesus said...But be BRAVE! John 16:33 ICB

Have you ever been scared to go someplace
new or do something different? _____
What does God tell you to do when you
are scared? _____

Draw a picture of a time when you were brave.

REMEMBER:

Jesus said... _____ be _____ . John 16:33

write your name   BRAVE

CONGRATULATIONS!

———————————————

HAS COMPLETED 21 DAYS OF KID CAN

I CAN DO ALL THINGS THROUGH CHRIST
WHO GIVES ME STRENGTH Philippians 4:13